Reaching V

Blessings
Kent —
in celebration
of happy times
of music &
poetry
together.
love Katie

ESSENTIAL POETS SERIES 210

Canada Council for the Arts **Conseil des Arts du Canada**

ONTARIO ARTS COUNCIL
CONSEIL DES ARTS DE L'ONTARIO
50 YEARS OF ONTARIO GOVERNMENT SUPPORT OF THE ARTS
50 ANS DE SOUTIEN DU GOUVERNEMENT DE L'ONTARIO AUX ARTS

Guernica Editions Inc. acknowledges the support of the Canada Council for the Arts and the Ontario Arts Council. The Ontario Arts Council is an agency of the Government of Ontario.

We acknowledge the financial support of the Government of Canada through the Canada Book Fund (CBF) for our publishing activities.

Reaching V

Kate Marshall Flaherty

GUERNICA
TORONTO • BUFFALO • LANCASTER (U.K.)
2014

Copyright © 2014, Kate Marshall Flaherty and Guernica Editions Inc.
All rights reserved. The use of any part of this publication,
reproduced, transmitted in any form or by any means, electronic,
mechanical, photocopying, recording or otherwise stored in a
retrieval system, without the prior consent of the publisher is an
infringement of the copyright law.

Michael Mirolla, editor
David Moratto, interior book designer
Guernica Editions Inc.
P.O. Box 76080, Abbey Market, Oakville, (ON), Canada L6M 3H5
2250 Military Road, Tonawanda, N.Y. 14150-6000 U.S.A.

Distributors:
University of Toronto Press Distribution,
5201 Dufferin Street, Toronto (ON), Canada M3H 5T8
Gazelle Book Services, White Cross Mills, High Town, Lancaster LA1 4XS U.K.

First edition.
Printed in Canada.

Legal Deposit – First Quarter
Library of Congress Catalog Card Number: 2013953825
Library and Archives Canada Cataloguing in Publication

Flaherty, Kate Marshall, 1962-, author
Reaching v / Kate Marshall Flaherty.

(Essential poets series ; 210)
Poems.
Issued in print and electronic formats.
ISBN 978-1-55071-834-8 (pbk.).   ISBN 978-1-55071-835-5 (epub).
ISBN 978-1-55071-836-2 (mobi)

I. Title. II. Series: Essential poets series ; 210

PS8611.L25R42 2014   C811'.6   C2013-907535-6   C2013-907536-4

I would like to thank: My loving parents, Ann and Dick, and my siblings, Richard and Kristin, who have all inspired me. My wonderful family, John, Annie, Gabriel, and Locky, who have filled my life with love and blessings. My creative and supportive poet friends, the Muse group, the Invisibles, and Voulez Vous poets, who have helped me fine-tune and polish. The Hot Sauce, Inkslingers and Sanctuary Sunday writers who have inspired and affirmed me, especially Sue and James. The brilliant musicians/composers, Mark and Cathy, who made the film and musical accompaniment for V, and Tony who imaginatively filmed. Mick Burrs, Liz Philips, Allan Briesmaster and Donna Langevin, whose eagle eyes, creativity and way with words all helped me to shape and edit this book. Michael Mirolla and Guernica Editions, for kind correspondences and for the gift of being published by such a fine press. The Light that shines through all poetry.

Contents

I. Goose, Plummeting

    Apocalypse of Bees *3*
    Skin *5*
    How to Slice a Mango *7*
    National Geographic Bookcase *9*
    Dark Waters *11*
    Goose, Plummeting *12*
    Reaching V *14*

Waiting Room *17*

II. Next of Kin

    I almost didn't write this poem *21*
    Next of Kin *23*
    Portrait of Self as a Bird *24*
    Egg and Ever *26*
    Grouse Medicine *28*
    Triptych for One Loon *29*
    Bear Totem *31*
    Painted Turtle *32*
    Sponge Poem *33*
    Mountain Meditation *34*
    Tadasana: Mountain Pose *35*
    Whale Medicine Card *37*

A New Language *39*

III. When the Kids are Fed

    What is Bagged in the Shed   43
    Breasts   45
    Jason's Mom   47
    Toronto Life   49
    Salted Poem   51
    Lining Up Ducks   53
    A Trio of Children   55
    When the Kids are Fed   57
    Changeling   58
    Locky, Ten Years Old, Leaning Closer   60
    Master of Handshakes   61
    Look to the Boneyard   62

Leaving Gold   63

IV. Practicing Like Water

    Practicing Like Water   67
    Marianna, Margaret, Marigold   69
    Far Away   72
    Adagio for Flute, Recorder and Piano   74
    Temple   79
    Voyageur   80
    Infinitesimal   82
    Photograph   84
    Funeral   85
    Eyes: A Triptych   87
    White Sheets   91

Drumming   93

V. Quicksilver

Quicksilver 97
Chimera 98
Feng Shui the Bedroom: A Five-Pointed Star 100
Meditation on Space 102
On Poets and Scar Tissue 104
Sugar Fast 105
Skrimhold of Reve 106
Dream in Slow Motion 108
The Randomness of Randomness 109
The Inner Wisdom of Objects 111

About The Author 113
Credits 114

I
Goose, Plummeting

Apocalypse of Bees

Some summers there were no frogs,
other summers, no snakes.

    One year there were no bees,
and Dad had the bright idea
of us kids pinching the pistils
from zucchini flowers
and squeezing them into their stamens.

    Even the strawberries
came out weird and misshapen.
The pumpkins looked like lopsided tumours.
The cucumbers were mere nubbins,
too small even for pickling.
And no butter squash at all.

        At the time, I resented doing bees' work.
I didn't want the prick-hot sun stinging my neck
the pollen-like snuff ragging my nose, nor
deer flies biting tiny chunks from my scalp.
I was not in the mood for flitting
from flower to flower in our parched garden.

Once again the bees are disappearing.

Today I read in the pallid paper
they are two-thirds gone
in Niagara Region vineyards.
Now there will be less table wine
with fewer bees to pollinate the grape blossoms.
Will we get shrivelled vegetables and puckered produce
with spindled swarms of bees to fertilize them?

My brain hums with scary thoughts
of shrunken fruit, shifting weather patterns,
a buzz of freakish storms —
May snow, bike rides at Christmas,
acid rain carving weird grooves into the Earth.

Eerie how this pattern homes in —
lonely honey makers in their empty hives,
busy workers, blue-dotted queens,
and pollinators
vanishing —

                bumbling into a new climate,
droning into silence.

Skin

In St Lucia the sun warms mango flesh,
its lush pungent fruit
mingling with hyacinth and seasalt.

My daughter's first word in Creole: *tété*.
She demands "Tay-tay!"
as she reaches for my breast
tumbling out of a sweaty sundress
like a melon spilling
from a market bag.

And all the women on the transport,
their natty braids in grids on their scalps,
pat my baby's soft blonde-tipped head
as if checking mangoes for ripeness.

Belly-laughing
with roosters trilling on their laps
at a white child speaking Patois.

Laughing deeper sweet juices, saying,
grose tété, bebe, mwe matche woo!*
while they hold their own
jostling breasts and breadfruit from town.

And my own provision
in a raffia bag on the rumble seat —
a tin of *soft candle* to spread on her chest
with camphor for a cold,
one woman telling me:
*feed the child ripe mango,
like healin' sunshine ...*

Palm trees blur past the steamy windows.

just peel back the skin
for mashin' the sunshine.

*Big boobs, baby, lucky you!

How to Slice a Mango

for cousin Ann

How to slice a mango
is something I learned
from my father's first cousin, the one
with piano-player's hands
and a Japanese surname with four syllables,
Yasuhara, like *origami*.

She folds notes into books she mails to me
and writes letters about sitting silent
and holding the light
at Quaker House meetings,
about her travels in Asia, about concerts
and the refugee boys she teaches.

When I ate her mango salad
with lime and a drizzle of sesame oil
at the Grand Haven beach house last summer,
the mango's peach-musk
fed a crowd of sun-parched cousins.

I asked her how she cut
the mango into tiny matchsticks.
But since the mangos were already cut
she had to show me how to do it
with words —
how to slice off both soft cheeks
and score them with a sharp knife
grazing the fibrous heart —
how to fold them gently inside out,
push up and pluck the juicy green-orange flesh.

And how in a ceramic bowl
she catches the nectar.

National Geographic Bookcase

In this dank wood cabinet I smell basement dust.
In the mildewed near-blackness I hear
the gentle squeak of door hinges
as I press my back to the bookshelf wall,

the yellow gloss
of a hundred National Geographic spines
luminous in the dark oak library.

Here I can close the doors to sighs,
sibling-noises and disconnected upstairs sounds.

Here I can think in the dim and silent sanctuary
and pore over the images:

An anaconda, fat as my waist, half submerged in water —
Aztec coins in a clay pot on sand — a nubile dancer

with a collar of bracelets propping up her long neck —
kerchiefed Roma children skipping in a circle on
    cobblestone —

an eagle's wingspan
               over a bald mountain.

These are my friends, who won't talk back,
who won't exclude me from secrets,
won't tattle-tale
               or shush up when I arrive.

My fascinating photogenic comrades
always wait where I left them
sitting on mats in a forest clearing,
leaning from stone hut windows,
smiling at me
with faces tipped towards the sun.

Dark Waters

My husband and the boys
are jumping off Hot Rocks in cannon ball tucks.
They shout savage sounds as they coil
and spring, hands clasping their knees.

Mom and I watch from our perch
on the warm quartz slope of the Bay
as they arc and splash into wakes from motor boats,
their wide eyes and open mouths making us laugh
as droplets reach us from each plunge.

It has been a cool sunless summer so far.
My partner's pike-belly body
seems pale in the root beer water.
He lolls languorously, like a mollusk unshelled,
smiling as he tilts his wet face to the rare-appearing sun.

What a contrast to the downtown dark suits,
the pinched-faces of Bay Street.
I look out over the sunny Sound,
notice one translucent crawfish caught in a crack of rock.

Goose, Plummeting

Look
and you might see the farmer,
his pails set down, gazing up
at the arrowhead flight-pattern of geese —
the precision-point leader heading
two lines in his wake.

The farmer rubs his muscles,
tight from the pull of pails, and marvels
at the grace of wings, communal flight.
His shoulders drop as he watches the perfect point
glide through the sky.
He thinks the word *wedge*.

A random shot
rips the silence,
then he witnesses the spiralling down —

one goose plummeting from its place
like ripped tar paper,
a ragged Valkyrie
descending
before the bird smacks the stubbled field.

A second goose pulls
from formation, spears
down to the mark.

Now the taste of storm is in the air.

It leads the farmer to the field
with a crate, water, his wife's wool blanket
for the grounded goose.

Her mate tenderly strokes
her splayed wing
with his beak.

The farmer cradles the wounded goose
in a sling of blanket
and carries her to the barn.
He looks back to nod at her partner,
who follows at a distance, blinking his bead eyes.

In a depression of hay,
her life-mate leans his curved neck onto her breast.

It will be only a day
until the she-goose expires.

After a night of nuzzling her dead body,
the goose flies away at dawn
to catch the draft of another V.

But years later the farmer still tells his wife:

"Every November
I swear that goose
pecks for a moment
at my barn window."

Reaching V

On this train, snow
wings past the window,
near strangers murmur,
and the Canada geese fly out of formation —
gone from my sight
by the time they reach V.
>Which is home for them?
>North or South?

Recalling this rest in their flight skein,
I think of you, Bev.
How illness plucks us
out of V-point,
scatters the pattern,
calls us to fall back
and rest on the draft, the current
of wings, to letting
each other take the lead
that cuts the harsh air.

>Dis-ease sends us to places of glass.
The enclosed hospital sunroom
where clear winds pierce dull clouds,
doubt curls the window with frost.
We look through the pane at the world
you would not re-enter as Bev.
You, the earth angel with swift feet.

You dream of riding the wind
and cry into my shoulder
on visits when words cannot lift your spirits.

Reaching V

Like the geese, we head home —
    faith the wedge that points the way —
leaning on lift,
trusting in our wingspan,
    listening in the silence of air
for the honk and the sweep
    of our feathers
        reaching V.

Waiting Room

I notice the pauses in my breaths
while I wait here and sense them
resting in this space
alighting like moths to a warm bulb.

They intuit the resting places
in waiting rooms
in decrepit corridors
in hospitals where someone has something
important to say.

They unfurl in the silent hallways
and hover above bed rests
where they interpret dreams.

Even when the body has begun to cease
spirits stay and wait.

II
Next of Kin

I almost didn't write this poem

scrabbling as I was for a piece of paper
or any scrap to write on before the name slipped
into folds of brain,
like a sliver of soap in the bath.

I almost didn't write this poem
but a yellow corner
of parking ticket was enough to jot the name:
Mariana (the tiny islands off India
that are shrinking as the oceans slowly rise.)

A sari'd woman said they will hold a *Scuba Summit* there —
men and women in wet suits under water
so members would know the feel
of silently submerging,
groping for breath,
vanishing.

(I get the bends just thinking about it.)

Watermarks on a map
erasing the name of a country.

I almost didn't write this poem
because the ticket was too small
for all the pencilled words
that spiralled into the margins.
I wrote smaller and smaller
'til I almost gave up.

I printed my name and address on the petition
wondering what words can do
to save the lowest land mass on earth.

But then a thought bubbled up:
I almost didn't write this poem,
whose last word is

Mariana.

Next of Kin

Moghur the Neanderthal medicine man
throws powder into the fire:
in the blue-bursts of flame
he sees far into a tunnel of smoke.

Chimpanzees share stick ladders
for ants to climb onto their tongues:
one chimp waves a stick in the air,
conducting a jungle symphony.

Cocoa the gorilla coddles
a kitten to her breast:
she puckers her lips softly
as if mouthing words.

And somewhere rests
a soft dark ape palm
hacked off and thrown
into a boneyard of ashtrays and elephant tusks.

Washo has been taught sign language.
He has learned to press his thumb
into his upper lip to make the *M* sound —
mama, me, mine.

Portrait of Self as a Bird

I. How the chickadee sees me

A poet stands in a slice of sunlight
on the seedy grass beneath the feeder,
listening with her whole body.
She has a notepad,
is trying to scratch down
the sounds of my cousins and I
as we twitter and tweak, streak
towards the sky.

She is mumbling,
"there is no alphabet"
for our song-sounds, *"no syllables"*
for the silence between celebrations.

When I cry out my name
in her language, she lights up
and scrapes the pencil
swiftly across the pad—
"Chick-a-dee-dee-dee-dee!"
I fly off the branch of an old crab apple
and land again, preening,
and peer over her pad to see
written: *"Birdsongs — more like a hinge,
these calls,
a tweek of wood on wood
or creak of tree.*

Except for the chickadee." I see her
see me, wonder: is she starting
to speak my language?
She of the strange sounds,
all affricates and glottal stops.

II. I am a chickadee

I am repeating
my end thrice
in a self-sung-song
on a jack pine branch.

My hermits' cap shines as I sing
in solitude this morning,
my black and white vestments
holy with dew-ness.

I crack open dawn.
I split sunflower seeds
to get to the soft heart
and the sweet meat.

Blinking my bead eyes at sunrise,
I raise my hymn of praise.

I know the secret
encoded in this text of tree —
these jack pine cones open
only when split by fire.

So I offer
these small burnt candles
to the morning — the ones with
the prayers tucked inside.

Egg and Ever

I. roost

Barnsmells of hay and chicken-shit
dried white like gypsum
    and dust-choke
underscore the hens churring
beneath the hot light bulb.

Some shuffle and crane their necks,
peck-hammer. Black eyes blink
    (caviar in feathers)
while some are still, the low trill
and guttural sounds of the brooders,
soothing as they roost.

II. cozy

Hens plume over the eggs
like preening tea cozies,
warming perfect ovals.

III. aglow

Hold the candle to an egg:
candle mass of light
to illuminate life
inside the yolk of potential —

this oval sphere aglow
in the dim barn-light,
sunrise arcing across a small planet.

Earth-egg —
in a pocketful of constellations
scattered like straw bits —

holding you in my palm
I am candling the world.

Grouse Medicine

I caught you drumming once
off the harvest road in fallen crimson,
your camouflage the russet golds of autumn.
Buried beneath leaves, your rumblings
stopped me, I pivoted in spirals
looking for the source of sound.

Then
a burst of fall chaff flew out,
there you were trembling, a-flutter!

I spied your red tympanum
in the drum-heat
blur of flapping wings,
and was not afraid.
The forest, a still backdrop for your pageant,
received your feathers,
dropped like judgments.

That day my vision of meditation
was sacrificed for the dance.

You are my spinning Sufi mystic.
In the centre of an orbiting tailspin,
you find stillness.

Triptych for One Loon

I.

Loon on the lake
past the salt docks and raked sand.

Suddenly there, the bird
has bobbed up further
from where it plunged — further
than imagined breath could be held.

Alone under the mid-day moon.

II.

Loon stays under so long
you almost forget he descended at all.
You turn back to your book on the beach

and then, like nostalgia, he comes
far from where you expected
he could go.

III.

Loon tilts his straight beak
and tucks his webbed feet for take-of —
flaps rhythmic wings that slap
down and up — loon and his wavy mirror-twin leaving
    a lean V trail.

       Disturbed water.

           Reading, interrupted.

Bear Totem

I must have walked past your cave,
my silent totem. I was ambling
through high rock forests of pine.
I felt I was searching as you were
for the honey of truth.

Once I crossed your grizzled brother
on the path to Beehive Mountain,
    I was startled—
and then he showed me
a way to leave and not cross him
on the switchbacks and *scree*.
But the swift paw of panic
still clawed at me.

Now I see:
the cave in rock, womb-like and warm,
filled with a soft cedar-bough bed.
Sweet smells of skin and grasses burning
just beyond imagining's horizon.

I am of your clan,
silent, and lumbering.
I know your secret fear—
you will sleep right through,
and, come spring, you will never awaken.

Painted Turtle

Stop the van!
we shout and slide out
from summer-stuck vinyl
like mollusks from a shell.

Look!
A painted turtle
with dry neck-cords stretched proud,
its claws curved as fine as eyelashes.
Blinking at us, it withdraws
its languorous head.

We roll it over with a stick,
touch the flat smooth squares
of its belly-armour, place it on the gravel shoulder,
our pop-jack puppet now locked in its box.
We gently rap on its curved roof:
Anybody home?

We wonder how it got so far from the gully,
what forest spirit tipped
a scarlet-orange Indian paintbrush
around its rim, and if it left
soft eggs by the water? Now who
will carry it back to the bulrushes, safe?

All ten hands make a gentle cradle
to return it to the spongy wet grass.
Laughing, victorious,
we cram back into the van.
*What would we have done
if it was a snapper?*

Sponge Poem

This urchin sea sponge
has gathered dust for years
behind the neglected shop glass.
Don't ask what kind of random shop this is.

Once there was a school of sponges
in the now-deserted place.
Today when kilted students pass,
leaning into the gritty wind,
they notice it is the only sponge left.

Next to this yellowing oval:
an ancient cement wedding cake
and a Caribbean poster with curled blue edges
proclaiming some relationship
more than mere proximity.

Never from behind this window
has leaked the pungent sizzle of chillies
wafting from other storefront cracks;
nor ever the base thump of reggae.

Yet the spiral of this vortex
soaks up all the grimy noises
of the city street.
And the sponge's withered pores
once ocean-drenched
now breathe in sound waves
like a bagged-out bagpiper,
a wimpled nun
who used to laugh out loud.

Mountain Meditation

From below, the snow-lined peak
splits a stream of clouds
so they plume and swirl around its tip.

I watch the peak's rugged cap vanish
into fluff and shadow.

The sunlight breaks through
in sliding shapes.

From down here
the tree-line looks like moss,
deep green and spongy.

When I ascend its bulk, I trace
a curving path as clay crumbles
under my hiking boots, my breath deeper
to draw oxygen in the thin air.

Heady with the ascent, I pause.
I could trip and slide down
the *scree*, lose my footing,
twist a limb, tumble off
a drop-dead ledge.

I stand still for a moment on the path.
The mountain knows where I am.
I am who the mountain is.
The mountain is earth pointing skyward —
like me, feet in clay, head in clouds.

Tadasana: Mountain Pose

I wake to snow
shocking on the railing
and luminous
in the pre-dawn purple
on the tip of Mount Rundle.
>*Stand at the top of your mat*
>*spread your toes to root the soles*

On Thanksgiving Friday,
this powder is sprinkled
here below
and on the startling peak.
>*Imagine roots unfurling*
>*to ground the feet*

Soon the sun will wink
over the hooded crown
of the mountain.
>*Draw earth energy up*
>*your two strong legs*

Mount Rundle re-awakens
under morning spreading
glint of gold.
>*Feel the heat rising in your belly*
>*as you breathe into your core*
>*mindful of* mullah bandha: *root lock*

Solar warmth slides
down the face
of solid rock.
>*Draw life into your belly*
>*awaken the breath:*
>*Inhale   Exhale*

The once-fired molten lava
now a stone heart.
> *You might feel the urge to run,*
> *get out of the pose —*
> *breathe and stay   breathe and stay*
> *this instinct to flee the colossal*

Grey.   Stone.   Monumental.
Huge heavy moisture-sucking mountain,
you stand firm and imposing.
I drop my jaw at your strict scowl.
> *Release the cleave of your tongue*
> *from the roof of your mouth —*
> *soften the clench of fear.*
> *Root the feet from fleeing the giant*

Mount Rundle,
you stand in storms,
weather the centuries
of abusing sky, crack
but not split in the harsh rays.
You remain firm,
your stable base unmoving.
> *Breathe in mountain air —*
> *drink in the posture of mountain*
> *remain erect   still*
> *the gale of restlessness*
> *will pass, a cloud*

Tadasana (ta-DA-sa-na): In hatha yoga, this asana or posture is a standing pose, tall and grounded like a mountain, with feet rooted in the earth and head high in the air.

Whale Medicine Card

Her blow hole
a fountain of seafroth:
water and breath.

Birthing calves in icy brine,
mother's milk in salt sea foam —
a cold blast of tears.
And her song
       and their song
              and our songs ...
echoes lapping.
The liquid sonar of history in waves.

Jonah in her belly.
Noah's ark, her rib's replica.
Mother Earth's librarian.
Mu is calling us land-dwellers
back to ancient ways.
Mammalia
       who slipped into liquid
             and still had breath.

She is calling to me —
signalling to me in dreams
the blue shoals of ancient waters.

Doubts jettison through the blow-hole —
    infinitesimal droplets into space.

I open my mouth
    to hear my heartbeat
        in the skin drum of my tympanum.
I long to sing
    our common song.
        Sounding, sounding the way
            out to open waters, and pure,
                so I'll not be beached again.

A New Language

for my son Gabriel

In the swell of my belly,
I first discovered you within me:
>*poke of tiny elbow-tip,*
>*strong kick*
>*in my ribs.*

I marvelled
>*when I ate bread*
>*I was feeding you also.*

I loved, leaned, let go in the dark.
>*I fumbled with words*
>*that could not go*
>*where I wanted them to —*
stumbling into a fresh dawning.

You came into the light
in such din and confusion —
surprised us as you were surprised.

Then sleeping amid harsh noises
>*your tiny ribcage*
>*rose and fell in waves*
swelling with newly-delivered promise.

>*Now we feel safe, somehow,*
>*sheltering you*
>*in this alien place.*

III
When the Kids are Fed

What is Bagged in the Shed

Poppa's trinkets shudder and rattle
against the window-pane
whenever one of the *grandkids* primes the pump outside.
They line up, tall and nervous on the sill:
an Alaskan fishnet float, the old-fashioned
spun sugar cone with its fancy crest,
and a camphor-smelling blue glass bottle.

Grandma calls him *packrat*,
the proof bagged in the shed —
yellowed curling papers, shiny photos
now sun-warmed into clumps,
nails and hooks on the mudroom wall
for a sun-bleached antler,
beaver jaws,
rusted horse-bit and buckle,
a holy minnow net,
the pale sienna of Georgian Bay sand.

We gasp at the tiny hummingbird nest
spun from cobwebs and the filament of moth feelers
light and sad as pipe smoke
which Rupert the trapper leaves behind
when he visits for permission to trap beaver, rabbit, lynx.

Poppa lets me touch the viceroy butterfly still
alive on his cap — the velvet powder wings,
bumblebee thorax, piece-of-thread legs
poking around like antennae.

It tickles.

Its wings open and close in tiny breath-beats —
now it's a brown paper scrap,
now a butterfly
in a blink.

Poppa's big hands
open the screen door to release the viceroy.

He offers me a half mussel shell
he found under his big chair —
a vessel for my new treasures.

Breasts

Full and sumptuous, I remember
having them in grade five,
much too large and always in the way,
trying to compress them with tensor bandages
like binding feet in China.

Gym class was a trickle of damp sweat between them,
snickers from outside the shower curtain,
"She's ... hitching up the team!"
while I fumbled to latch the trainer bra.
Julia Bower with her sleek, flat, boy-figure
could dance naked,
squirting water at the other girls.
Everyone laughing.
I just sat on the bench,
feeling fat, and trying not to gape.

The tan smouldering Grade Eight twins,
Warden and Clyde, would gaze
at them, and not my face, in the hall.
I'd want to duck down
and catch their eyes: *Hello, I'm here!*
But I could only stare, hot-flushed, at the floor,
pull down my kilt.
Hugging my books tighter.

Summer hot shorts and halters were "in"
for all the club-house girls,
dirt-sure in their clapboard fort —

Only me
in my baggy sweatshirt
picking grass outside the fence,
whispering to myself they were simply jealous,
day-dreaming about a wax figure of my body
I could carve perfect.

Jason's Mom

Jason's basement is a dank-smelling
magical dungeon under an artists' lair —
We find tiny maquettes
of a fairy merry-go-round
with a bright parachute top,
a miniature guillotine
with an angled slice of foil
and a small kitchen under a Christmas bulb.

I don't want to go home,
want to stay here and drink *Beep,*
eat licorice and skip lunch,
walk my fingers in a Lilliput set,
try on the royal velvet cape,
wield the ruby talking stick,
fit my toes into the sequined
Peter Pan getaway shoes.

This is the land of make-believe,
of old-fashioned hats, spells
and secrets, far from rules and vegetables.

Jason's Mom has polio,
walks with an aching lurch,
paints in the garden,
calls him "lover" and kisses him on the face —
tells me I'm a good girl,
and he's her prince.
Lets us touch his father's
Stratford stage sets,
play with props.

When I sleep over, she asks me what I mean
when I tell her we say prayers at night,
throws her head back with a silken scarf:
"How sweet! How delightful!
Tell us one right now!"
(Like it might be a spell, a charm,
or an incantation) —
she makes *me* feel like the magician.

Toronto Life

Once there was an article in *Toronto Life*
featuring our Easter Egg tree
in the "Things to See About Town" section.
In the seventies, no one else had such a tree.

All those weekends we sat around the dining room table
with newspapers spread out
under the tarnished twists of our chandelier
where the eggs hung to dry.

Paints, beeswax, dyes, lacquer and little fingers
all made eggshells into art.
We suspended our shiny spheres
from the trees every Easter,
then wrapped them in tissue
and boxed them in the hall closet year after year,
their wool loops stiff with paint
varnished on the fragile orbs.

The old magnolia proudly displayed the eggs
once its soft April petals had fallen to the pavement.

The tree was so laden
with oval ornaments on its knotty branches
there was barely space for the golden *Alleluia* goose egg.

Then one year some bullies picked off
most of our treasures
with slingshots.
My Dad cried unabashedly
when he opened the door Easter morning
to see smashed pieces on the sidewalk
and jagged half-shells clinging to the trees.

Our sour neighbour shouted:
"It was them Jewish kids that done it!"
But we knew it could not have been
the orthodox and soft-hearted Kravitz kids.

We were left wondering about eggshells and brokenness.

It got us into questioning:
What kind of mood would want to shatter beauty?
What kind of mind would blame the Kravitz kids?

My father never hung another egg tree after that.

We were left to wonder
which was worse —
To smash special eggs in the night?
Or to blame a scapegoat first thing in the morning?

Salted Poem

in memory of Stephanie Gardner

The sun's stark noon brightness
dazzles my salted eyes
as we bake ourselves
on terry towels at Jersey Shore.
Me and my "not-quite-cousins."

The girls are older than I am,
and eat diet yogurt in cups by the shore.
They show me how to squeeze lemon into my hair
to make highlights
as we walk for miles along the beach to get an even tan.
In town they pick out a boutique shirt for me
and one gem hairclip I wear with pride.

They are beautiful —
past adolescent awkwardness —
safely settled into their glowing bodies
while I am still acclimatizing to mine.
Their string bikinis striking and not at all self-conscious,
while my one-piece creeps up in places,
and gapes, glumly, in others.

They grind course sea-salt onto their salads from a glass mill.
I've never seen salt being ground like pepper.
Their beach home is all glass and salt air too,
like a clear round cellar with a wooden base,
picture windows with golden oak floors and beams.
The azure sky and puff clouds surround us.

It is like heaven here —
light summer foods with delicate seasonings,
highlighted hair, bright adult banter that includes me.
I feel the sprinkle of fine sea-sand on the wooden floors
as I tip-toe towards young womanhood.

P.S.: A few years later,
Stephanie, the youngest sister,
wrote us a letter about Jersey Shore —
the sun's brightness,
the year's blessings,
and her promising life.

Then she went sailing
through the van's windshield
like a seagull smashing glass.

A fierce light
shattered into fragments.

Lining Up Ducks

for Kristin

You always say: "Let's line up our ducks!" —
meaning to set up a picnic,
or a frolicking spot for the kids,
or a stop-for-tea place.

I imagine a flat of cut-out duckies at the Fall Fair —
teenagers peering through sights
to pick them off in a row —
    yellow ducks tilt, pinging *one two three!*
and laugh at the sister-lingo of it,
knowing just what you meant:
lining up our ducks.

But this afternoon under lazy low-slung clouds,
I listen to the crackle of gravel and kayaks
dragged into the still lake.
I hear the cricket chorus,
the breezy oak-leaf and odd
dropping acorn pop,
and I imagine your laugh
as I peer over my notebook.

I see a mallard leading her eight fluffy ducklings
in a perfect evenly-spaced straight line
across the tranquil water.

I marvel at this mother
heading the parade so proudly,
never looking back
to check on the chicks
in their bridesmaids' regiment,
and recall that silly expression
for ordering, getting straight, symmetry.

Mother duck quacks
her uproarious laugh: *wa waa waaa!*
and glides on.

I am struck — I've just glimpsed
one of nature's intricate plumb lines.

A Trio of Children

I. Before Waking

for Locky

He told me he thought he heard music —
washing up as waves
from the downstairs piano where his brother practiced
Stephen Heller's "Prelude in D Minor."

He wondered were they *real* melodies wafting into his dream,
or dreamscapes so musical they *seemed* real?

I saw his fingers rippling slightly over the sheets
    as if tinkling invisible ivories,
        his shallow breath, rhythmic and undulating.

        The music slid over the stark sands of
waking, blurring the harsh rocks of the beach.

II. Playschool

for Gabriel

He sits alone, he doesn't fit
the playschool mold.
His mother watches him build a stacking toy,
wonders if she can hold this fragile boy
as he grows his own backbone?
She struggles to make sense
of his longing to line things up,
stands astounded
at his inner symphony.
His pain of looking on
from a solitary place
slots
into her own.

III. Origami

for Annie

It is now time for her first-born child
to set sail on the reflecting stream.

She pushes her child gently out, a paper boat,
and blows a soft breath
at the fragile, folded vessel.

When the Kids are Fed

After the weeding and wilting, bean-
snapping, brown-soap-and-vinegar'd bug bites —
    After the trip in a hayseed van to the co-op
for duck feed and a candy stick,
the jars of "garden special"
neatly lined up in the root cellar —
    After the hike to the sugar shack
past the few forlorn fruit trees
felled by the she-bear —
    After a peasant supper of soup and bread,
Gramma's mile-high strawberry shortcake,
the scrap over dish duty,
a few rounds of 99 —
    Now the kids squeak in the bunk-beds above me
as I sit in the window rocker watching
the return of the red-winged blackbird
to his oily twig; the chaos of the day
settling under the steady watch of the Big Dipper —
    And I dare not lean or shift
in my rocking chair, but I stay
still beside the picture window,
watching the pearl moon
illuminate a peony, its petals in a pile
beside the old pump.

Changeling

for Gabriel

I named you after the angel who announced:
*Something is coming to Earth
like you've never known before.*

Sometimes you are not
the little boy who'd squeeze
me in a deep-squeeze hug,
line up pasta on the floor,
draw crayon pictures of God.

Back then you'd lean into my
wisdom like a rose trellis.

You said once as we poked raisins
into the soft sternums of gingerbread boys:
I thought aliens were angels, Mom.

Sometimes teenagers
seem like they're from outer space.

I pray to your guardians
when I read about the effects
of electro-magnetic waves on the brain,
and gaming thumb syndrome,
or the wreckage of Facebook gossip.

You said then as you twisted the dough into rings:
*I'll bet the creatures in UFOs
have evolved past what we are, eh Mom?*

Reaching V

Sometimes we earthlings
do squander our pearls.
You, using your piano fingers for techno gaming —
me, scribbling to-do lists instead of poems.

We wonder at portents in the sky,
each shining star lost in a scatter of lights.

Locky, Ten Years Old, Leaning Closer

A brown hoodie lies sodden in the gutter
as we walk to school in the drizzle, holding hands.

We both look into the sewage grate swollen
with leaves and mud. You point to a plump earthworm
beside the sloughed-off sweatshirt
like a shed skin. It looks to me like your hoodie —
you say it looks to you like the worm will
somehow tunnel into the woven cotton.

We stand over this soft, wriggling
creature. The oily leaves on
wet branches hang over our heads.
Your palm is warm and soft.

We lean closer. You squat and peer —
like you did as a solid toddler, reverent,
not disturbing the creature's earnest efforts
to find safety — absorbed in its movement,
moist skin, urgent mission.

I think
how vulnerable is this worm, trying to dig
into what is not earth.

I look at the pink worm, the hollowed shadow
in the nape of your neck. How fragile
your exposed skin, streaked with strands of wet hair,
everything clinging.

Master of Handshakes

"Come on lucky seven!" he sings out,
as our two hands ripple
and slap each others like fish.
We laugh through his ritual
before every hockey game.

He is Master of Handshakes —
has a bee-bop, fingertip slide, back
to back, scoop step and slap
with his seventeen-year-old sister and
a smash top, one potato, two potato, three potato,
four knuckle-crack and sternum-pop
with his fifteen-year-old brother.

He calls them "*secret* handshakes"
but they are brash and noisy and public. Like him —
with his operatic "Laaa...ta-da!" entrance
onto every stage.

Yet there is a secret part
like a hidden pocket
to his outlandish out-there-ness.
At ten, he still rubs the tattered ear
of his teddy, presses the button nose
close to his cheek, rubs his scissoring fingers
over Ted's patched and balding fur —
says he loves the bear
"because
he smells of soap, like you."

Look to the Boneyard

for John

And if I were to die
suddenly, without a chance
to rest in my gratitude,
I'd regret so many things unsaid,
so many pages unturned.

I would have left a note:
Look to the boneyard
for shiny phrases,
for praise sounds and word pearls
found along the way —

All those orphaned gems
not having found their place
in poems yet —
unpolished, waiting
for a soft chamois to rub them clean.

Look to the boneyard, temporary
resting place for jewel-tops
that poke out like ruby turnips
waiting to be excavated, unearthed
from the field of things unsaid.

Look. There you'll find
your own name, too.
       It was you who held me
       as I turned
       those diamonds in the light.

Leaving Gold

She knew — only six years old,
her disorder had more syllables
than her alphabet blocks —
she simply knew.

She began to leave hidden epistles
long before her story would end.

Little scraps of foolscap tucked into teacups·
and the chink in the pot of the weeping fig.

Ripped pictures
and drawings rolled into tiny tubes,
inserted like stoppers into soil, seams, pockets, shoes.

Mementos under the mat,
swept like beach sand.

Pasted artwork slipped under the bed
to ward off nightmares.

What mother seeing her precious coin missing
wouldn't sweep clean the house,
throw open the shutters
in search of her lost gold?

Tiny reminders —
bits of newsprint with her name
scrawled in bold crayon —
bright as the slant of sun in the kitchen —

scraps of love still found like golden leaves
months after her funeral.

IV

Practicing Like Water

Practicing Like Water

I.

Crumbs of sleep in my eye.
Dream residue.

I squeeze my lids tight,
burrow deeper
into the warm blanket-folds,
wanting to go back
where I am sharing a meal with you
at a sunny pine table.
Cascade Mountain through the glass.

No need to speak,
or hold hands,
peaceful silence dissolving
into one smile like water.

II.

The weightless feeling still fluttering
in the cage of my ribs.

Why do we waken
with such longing, sometimes?

Have we been floating with angels?
Practicing for death,
in sleep?

Are we slipping into a pool
where dream and dreamer are one?

Are we each a cup of water
poured into the sea?

Mariana, Margaret, Marigold

for M.W.

I. M is for ...

Margaret, even before your email,
Bev's appearance in my dreams
seemed important, a sign, some deep reminder.

Her face was animated and as beautiful
as I remember it — dark bangs brushing
her freckled forehead and gray-green eyes
brighting out from a rim of lashes.
And her mouth was moving in my dream
with kind words: "I've missed you ..."

Yes. Yes, I thought, and it didn't strike me as odd at all
that her head would speak to me
from inside a goldfish-bowl space helmet on the floor.
No more painful body —
or was the earth now her trunk and limbs?

I was so happy to see her droll smile,
hear her low voice.
The watcher, watching me dream,
knew Bev died over two years ago,
and yet here she was
once more speaking to me
with soul-torquing urgency.

A warm hum of longing rose in my throat
and I found I was crooning
as the watcher and the watched then merged
and morning crested. I awakened
to feel her near.

I will remember to call on her, our beloved Bev,
to sort out how to respond.
I will read past the reeling I feel once again.

I recall how you and I met, Margaret,
and became friends by her deathbed,
seeing that same metamorphic
M-word in your email now.
Malignant.

II. There will be no regrets in this death poem

> *with thanks to Priscila Uppal*

There will be no regrets in this death poem
like seeds irritating the soft bellies
of oysters
waiting to be pearled

There will be no seeds in this death poem
like the chaff separated from the sheaths of wheat
scattered on the hard ground
awaiting a sower

There will be no hard ground in this death poem
no earth so packed it cannot be split open
for the planting of magnolia bulbs
shoots unfurling
up and down

There will be no bulbs in this death poem
no flashes of light or stars in the eye or shocking footage
    of life
passing before your eyes in a second

There will be no stars in this death poem
no constellations to wish on
no heroes or villains
no understudies rehearsals or prima donnas —
just this one chance

yet
there will be no chance
in this death

only seed-bulb slits like points of incense
pressed into earth soft as wax
regrets bee-spun into honeycomb lessons
of healing and letting go

I did not say there would be no pain

Far Away

Your pictures taped on the wall,
tenderly showing the proper sequence —
panties before skirt, socks before shoes — set me
wondering what an Alzheimer's mind
feels like inside ...

Grandma, I place myself in your frail frame,

scrolling back to my own childhood
where daughters seem sisters,
sleepwalkers startle and wake
under snowy lamp-posts,
where I think I must know you but
your name dissolves like tissue in a tub.

Such a mind
is like a stalwart mule
refusing the harness and cart,
the ox cart, oxo cubes, *x's* and *o's*, hugs and kisses;
signatures flattening to a scrawl.

And this once was poetry with words like luminous.

They say you stew in your own brain juices.
If you were sweet you would thicken; if sour,
then you are Old Sneep sucking on a lemon.

How is it amnesia doesn't wipe away language?
The life-story forgotten but not the words.

We lost the way but not the meaning of: I am lost.

Aren't we all lost?
And shuffling down the corridor vague
as melting clocks, dilly dally,
daily times and doorknobs.
Opening the tin and sons becoming brothers,
names falling away
like flesh from soup-stock bones.

Lily pad thoughts float on murky ponds,
white and clean as daisies on a gurney,
chalk-white like the nurses' sensible shoes.

Or fingernails screeching on a slate,
black hole sucking in everything like a Hoover,
an eight-ball rebounding but never sunk.

And sometimes, after long days of staring at
nothingness:
a nameless child emerges, and offers a lemon square,
and stands close to you ... as close as memory.

Adagio for Flute, Recorder and Piano

I. Blow, North Wind.

Clear away
what we no longer need.

Whisper your cool hush
into our ears. Your exhalation
is our inspiration.

Tip our heads to look up
for the bright winter goose
above the snow line,
for signs in stars.

Breathe again through our fields,
shush away the chaff.

You who spin the windmills
and puff proud sails,
fill the socks on the line, move
chimes to their tinkling songs
of glass, air, space.

Grandfather wind
you are wise and bring in change,
not always harshly, but soft
as your tuft of white beard.

Your wind-tunes shatter the stillness
like clean falling icicles.

You may howl, wild and blustery,
and force me to run in the harsh air,
but I will only spit and stammer.

I want to lay down my shivering spear,
gently, so you might
let the flute of my body
make music of your flowing through me.

II. Half-Rest

Playing my pine recorder,
I see a tiny *z*
floating at the end of a line
in the bar, a hovering
half rest —

not even a full rest,
hanging big-bellied, slung
low under the belt —
only a demi-breath, a pause,
just enough air for me
to finish the musical phrase.

This half-rest floats above me, waiting
for a place to light like a luna moth.

Is it a semi-pause caught up
in the vortex of children's demands and revving engines —
a fleck of dust sucked
into my city's noisy vacuum?

Or is it just a spindly insect drawn to heat?
Or a crooked bird on a current of air?
Or a bumbling bug strung on a line
in a spidery web?

Decorating the score
this miniscule *z*
sprouts a fiddlehead fern's curl,
hanging on as if too frail to stick.

A rest is just a sniff,
    a snippet,
        a whiff—
a break in the pace,
a crack in the arrangement
before the cacophony before the rest of my life resumes.

III. Cumulonimbus

    1.

She plods a sad song on the piano.

A storm is rolling in,
thick and crushing gray.
Cumulonimbus clouds are gathering—

papers and scholarship hopes
rest in a pile on the bench
beside her wads of wet tissue.
Her head bows under the weight of University.

2.

I remember when Annie was just a toddler,
her face tipped up during storms in St. Lucia,
which brought more cloying heat, not relief.
Hibiscus popped red out of the steam,
swollen gutters flooded the transport stop in
 Castries,
cardboard roofs from clapboard shanties
bumped soggy into the curb's flood grates
during the grey green deluge.

Astounded by the sudden rip
in the laden cloud-hammocks,
she would clap and jump
as we ran screaming for shelter.

In Derek Walcott Square,
under the huge and gnarled baobab,
she would point to the swollen sky,
electric with lightning, and shout:
"Stop now!
We've had enough!"

We would wait it out — listening
to other children's screams, to splashes
of water on tin roofs, to thunderclaps
smacking the wet sky,
and to rivulets of rain
hitting gutter grates.

Then the storm's sudden halt,
and hush after the last clap.

3.

Now, hearing Annie sigh
makes me think how heavy
the cloud of expectations can be.
I see the stack of books beside the piano,
the lightning speed of change it represents.

She whispers once more: "Enough,"
and then resumes her playing.

Temple

Bengali yogi tips hands to lips,
a house made of people?
He stands in the sun, sinewy,
his white wrap stark
against his caffa skin.

    A body is a temple, yes —
bars of ribs to keep the heart un-struck,
two portals of breath,
two windows of light
and a long red welcome mat
for nourishment —
the dome of the crown in the clouds,
the root of the soles in the earth.

Yes, the body a holy place, a home:
    I ruminate:
        "We borrow these clothes ...
        light looks different
        on the stoop or the shrine ...
        but it is the same light."

A house made of people?

So many bones —
so many broken windows
and shuttered eyes,
so many human stones on this earth —

a house of people — impossible —
without love as mortar.

Voyageur

You took me on my first portage
through Magnetawan and French River.
We packed trail mix, coffee, hunks of cheese,
matches and a map in plastic
flattened across the top of our pack.

I loved your canoe's birch ribs.
You taught me to craft
j-strokes, slides and dips
with my smooth wooden paddle.
We lurched in gentle unison on the river,
watching the droplets make v-trails behind us.

I remembered school words: *drumlin, esker, delta, fault,*
and felt a deep relief within me
as I became part of the legend on this map.
I watched the contours become rock lift, cliff,
or a stand of leaning jack pines, remembering
the Group of Seven's tree silhouettes.

I breathed in sulfur match-strike, wood-smoke
and damp watermarks on the map
we'd fold and unfold 'til some creases became slits
we could see the river through.
We caught the scent of bullfrog and sweat
as the sun baked our back-skins
and bounced off the river in bright sparkles.

Reaching V

When I feared we were lost
as one scraggly pine in rock island
looked like the next,
you pointed at the paper —
creased and grease-marked from travel —
and announce to the mighty Magnetawan:
"We are here."

Infinitesimal

this is not about the big picture,
the overview
the forest for the trees
or even the light within them all

this is not about science
       or space
              or speculation

this is about trying to imagine
the almost inconceivably
smallest unit,
where words fall off
the spectrum of possible description
just

imagine your hand,
the bones, the blood, the cells, the atoms,
the electrons spinning in their tiny orbits

then imagine the light in the electron

then break the pinpoints of light
into the infinite invisible
bits of bits of bittiest bits:

    QUANTUM —

the word like a chant
or an ancient sutra

two soundless syllables
un-clapping

almost unbelievable
but for *the feeling*

Photograph

The grainy sepia snapshot of your shining face
hangs, mounted on a plaque,
at the Interfaith Centre where I work.
Wisps of hair curl above your slim shoulders.
Your slender neck and chiselled chin rise
from a too-big woollen overcoat;
you gaze somewhere over my head.

I cannot recall this picture's date — and wonder
was it taken after Peter Van Pels
tenderly brushed your cheek?
After a night of murderous silence? After
a hundred days of hiding in the stifling attic?

There is no sign
of tragedy in this likeness of you —
your eyes like clouds in two rims of light, shiny
port-holes looking out to sky and sea.

Larger-than-life size,
this photo is projected often
onto the shadowy scrim
like a silent film
flashing black and white
in my dreams.

While the details of your visage
are hard to recall as I chase them
like a chip of eggshell in slippery white,
your words remain clear: "Despite everything
that has happened, I still believe
people are really
good at heart."

Funeral

My sister begins reading, then pauses.

The church, silent as stones, waits
while she stands
still at the podium under a granite angel.

I feel the keen swell of mother-loss now —
as my sister pitches her voice into the words.
Unable to peg down the line of tears,
she falters at the word *tent*.

I see the four banners
hanging from the corner pillars —
black, red, white, and gold —
people of wind, grass, river, flame
who carried their homes on their backs.

Watching my sibling treading carefully
on stepping-stone words,
the current of emotions swirling round,
I imagine wanderers
gathering hospitality into bundles:
food from the earth, beauty in the wild
scatterings of flowers.

I think of her mother-in-law,
now spirit,
who carried her dreams across the sea,
scattered seeds and sprinkled sweets,
who moved with grace
through a briefer autumn
than we might have wished —
but full of deep russets and gold.

The scent of love baking by the hearth
while she pitched her tent among us.

Eyes: A Triptych

I. Scanning

I flee my desk, flee my computer,
slog across the city in the February slush —
only to stare in a café at blank pages.
I watch people confide
into their cell-phones,
talking to air.

"No, I'm alone," says one guy
above all the chatter of voices.
I feel strangely affronted —
I am here, yet
feel guilty for listening in,
pretending not to be.

I think of my own creeping coagulation of words —

All the journaling no one will read,
just lines and circles to connect brain, blood and ink.

Sometimes I listen in and jot things down
as if scanning for a penny in the snow.

I sift through images within this frosted window,
    icicle spears suspended from its ledge,
        glaciers dragging stones across the eons,

            I try to prime the frozen pump of my brain
              waiting for a thought.

II. Shaping

for Gabriel

Our footprints tamp the snow under the stark moon
on the longest night.
The crisp air tingles our cheeks, bites
sharply in our lungs.

You shape a handful of snow into a ball that bursts
into pins of light fluff, snow too cold
to pack. Your shadow slides
long over the smooth ridge of white,
lean in the haloed moonlight.
It is rare when you and I walk in the clear night.

Your breath makes a swirl of frost-smoke.

Today someone mentioned how clay on a potter's wheel
must be pliable, ready, open — just the right warmth
to be malleable in firm hands.

Tonight you let me rest my arm on your shoulder.
How rigid your strong spine,
how angular your jaw, how taut
the ridges of ribs and sinew in your torso.
You stand taller than I now, talk back, argue,
resist, or just leave your cracking voice suspended
in the icy sheen. Standing erect in the snow,
more man than boy, you stare
hard past the bare trees.
But in the liquid of your eyes
I see a spark of moon.

III. Unblinding

1.

This cold winter day bites the tip of my nose into red
pins
and makes visible my breath
as living hoar frost.

I lean against a shop window
to face the sparkling sun, squint
and blink in the dazzle.

When I close my eyelids,
sun and veins mix into a blood orange
glowing inside each retina.

I imagine this colour is what I am seeing
with my eyes closed.

2.

and I hated the scene
when the villain scooped out Gloucester's eyeballs
like picnic watermelon.

Shakespeare's most hateful words to me: "Out vile jelly!"

That scarring image of wiping gelatin off rough thumbs.

But I knew my unacknowledged hero
then had insights even when blindfolded.

Now my scowl melts like warm wax
in the March sun, and I see how speed
tightens the blinders.

3.

A Ugandan friend had river blindness —
tiny river fleas eating away at vision —

How we race to be done with winter,
How we long to look past the gray.

If I interpret the sun long enough and then open my eyes,
the world becomes lime green like spring.

Then I see why happy are those
who cannot see
yet still believe.

White Sheets

for Bev Peake, (Jan. 28, 1956 to Sept. 4, 2006)

Her startled awakening
from a morphine sleep:
shock of eyes alight,
drawing me close,
a breath-whisper:

> *You were in my dream!*

Radiance from her pale chemo'd face
made my heart burn within me
(why was I not afraid?)

Her flushed face vibrant
against the tousle of white hospital sheets
and a cotton bedspread from the cottage.

> *You and my long-gone Virginia.*
> I saw all her beloved on a porch,
> splendid with sunlight.

She shone as she recalled
the sheets on the line so dazzling.

Luminosity in wind.

> *I was serving soup.*
> *The amazing sun.*
> *Enough for all...*

I want to go back there!

Wild eyes and peace at once —
and me wanting to crawl
into this comfort place for her, for me —
to see those flapping angels on the line.

Drumming

for Nelson Mandela

In here, there is sound:
>*keys clink against belt clasps,*
>*spoons scrape on canteen trays,*
>*rasps of iron grating*
>*half-words, swearing, Swazi, Afrikaans and*
>*hacks of spittle-splats on cement.*

And within that, a non-sound —
>*so negative-sounding, so zero, it hums electric in*
the inner ear after lights out, a ring in the brain like after
a sonic blast, or that audible sting of having stood too
close to a loud speaker.

>*Grief, a rusted hinge, opens wide*
>*throughout the night.*

>*Slam of metal gate. Slam of metal gate.*

And after that:
>*white noise.*

>*We can't imagine where you are confined as we*
are in Solitary but at the appointed hour as the sun sinks
over this scorched dungeon you merge with us drumming
with a spoon on iron bars.

>*Beats quicken in every cage.*

V
Quicksilver

Quicksilver

I am afraid of poisons
leaching from factories.
I hear the tinkle of my own silvered voice,
a teaspoon in a glass beaker —
an experiment with freakish sediment
all stirred up.

Mercury is clouding my purity.
Steam rising; nothing is clear.

Chimera

I.

I saw a photo once in *The Star*
of twins, conjoined at the crown,

waiting to be surgically separated.
Would only one live? A host

of questions my mother couldn't answer:
Why pull apart siblings? And how?

Now I might ask, were they two eggs
in one womb fused? Or one split?
Recalling tales:
unions of two creatures,
goat and man, woman and fish,

one with cloven hooves,
one, a split tail-fin.

II.

Me, the eldest of three, with my own name.
Twins in Gambia are always *Adama* and *Howa:*

First and Second — the same flesh
and bone, same sign under the stars.

Satyr or mermaid,
one will lead, one will yield.

Two swanlike spines spooning in a womb
sucking each other's thumbs *Adama. Howa.*

III.

But these infants, a pair of stars
fused in a dark sea,
protecting and sharing one pearl.

The Parents chose
the boy-child, not the girl.
I could not find the justice in it

Light paying a remittance to shadow.

Feng Shui the Bedroom: A Five-Pointed Star

a partially found poem

Point One:

Welcome the tranquil
healing energy of restful hues.
Brush with calming colours —
cream slip of lily, velvet puff of lavender,
soft labia of tulip.

Point Two:

Place silent bed
in a *commanding position*
far from the entrance
with one eye on the door
to witness and welcome
the flow of healing chi.
Leave space for a sigh
release the world beyond the doorway.

Point Three:

Soften the "poison arrows"
of sharp angles and points
with plants of cascading greens,
round curves, and drapes of fabric —
silks softening the knee,
or a head surrendering harsh thoughts
to the plush of pillow.

Point Four:

Clear out all clutter.
Throw open the shutters!
Let the cool wind
sweep away cobwebs, a mint-
fresh and shocking blast,
leaving your cottage,
sanctum, swept clean; simple
as a hermit's —
and as peaceful.

Point Five:

Treasure the room
as a sensual haven
with scents of *neroli* and *ylang-ylang*,
tranquil orange blossom,
touch of pussy-willow,
glimpse of gold thread in a tassel
or sapphire glitter of jewelled bead.
Arrange for the faint scent of musk,
pine breeze in the sheets.

Feng shui the room,
the temple of your spirit.

Meditation on Space

*Modern science now knows what sages of old
have always known that, in the body,
there is more space than matter.*
— Tony Murdock, *Towards Stillness*

I consider the space between atoms,
then think of the gaps in things.

My thoughts leaping across the rift
between synapse and dendrite,
my breath playing through emptiness,
chasms in communication
when no words bridge the divide
between us.

What do I make space for in my life?

Reflection:
filling of my pauses with pondering.

Sleep: the dreamscape
where my images can float
in a vacuum of nonsense and memory.

Walking in nature:
in open fields under endless sky,
I see pockets of forest in the dense and droning city.

Silence:
the pause at the top of my breath —
longing for the inhalation to escape,
to sing out a breathy tone:
exhale, let go, make
even more space

for meditation on space.

On Poets and Scar Tissue

How the two fester at odds with each other,
poets and scar tissue.
The poet pulling off scabs, peeling back
the layers and scrubbing the skin raw;
the scar tissue glazing over the wound,
smoothing the suture, bridging the cut.

Imagine sticking the words onto paper,
stitching them on, tacking to keep them from tumbling
off the page and into soft fissures.
How can they enter the organs,
if not through the cracks?

This modern fascination with laser surgery,
scouring wrinkles, hiding age-lines, tucking in bulges!
Poets want to gut the fish, rip open the stuffing,
scoop out the pumpkin-guts, let things
hang where they will.

The healing in the opening.

Word-salve from wounds.

Sugar Fast

This is harder than rock candy,
broken into brittle bits
with each bite;
sharper than those cones at Pioneer Village,
rolled in paper and stamped with a crest;
more nebulous than the pink batten spun at a circus
that leaves a tacky beard.

I am astounded at how I crave it, find it
hidden in odd places —
how I seek bliss in sifted measures.
    Such strange stirrings.

The old sprinklings no longer satisfy.
Artificial sweeteners are bitter with weird after-tastes.
The smell of sweet boilings soon turns sickening.
Then a thought rises like a bubble in viscous taffy —

I realize I've been super-saturated
with appetite and addictions to treats
and other candy-coatings, but
with each sugar-free day

there is a sweet dissolving,
a cleansing of palette,
awakening of taste buds
as I stick out my new tongue
(dreaming of strange feasts) —

this incredible nectar
    ambrosia
        slowly fulfilling within.

Skrimhold of Reve

I.

By day she's a delusional thinker
to imagine x will save y
but here in this place of transition
anything goes

Falling through that thin
membrane of wakefulness
she slips into ancient times
as if a fairy queen
poured dream-liquor into her eyes

She sails on brigantine waves
sees far-off lands
through a silken skein

She can wear her medieval cone-hat
with its gauzy mane
speak to trees in their
secret sister language
or wish on a five-pointed star

Her night-ship sails through
shoals of pastel corals
and shimmering silverfish

through the watery gates of earth-sea
to bliss

II.

She becomes Nils the goose-boy at night
recalling the Netherlandish fairy tale
about the boy who soared on the back
of a white goose

feathers fall from the air
and land on her pillow
stirring her sleep just enough to lift the veil
so she thinks *I am watching my own dream!*

III.

The dreamer mutters in her own *rem* language
that this place
is not unlike the land of nod

not unlike the wavering water-reflection
of a wedge of geese in clouds
where the leader points the way for a while
encouraged by the honks
of all the others in their V-shape

not unlike mist on a marsh
where you cannot quite tell water from sky

Dream in Slow Motion

Across the river
lotus boats float in olive water.
I am watching the tower
of bamboo stilts stretch up
to the dusthot Vietnam sky.

The dream drone of locusts
serenades the lily junk ladies.

But as if in slow motion,
the top builder tips a bucket
which topples to tilt a plank
from which another worker is tossed like a bug
down to hit a lower beam
that bumps a builder
that startles a stay wire
that sends another plummeting ...

Like fish weights descending slowly,
men drop.

I am helpless, a pillar of salt,
separated by a chasm. And a river.

Lily petals plop to the water
while my mouth hangs open.
One man flips like an acrobat
to land on the ground, erect,
as amazed as me
and the other bent women of the water.

The Randomness of Randomness

OK, I'll try one random poem
about two talkers saying the same word
at the same time and one must then shout: *jinx!*
or a winning lotto ball
    tumbling into the televised lottery slot
or a bird hitting skyscraper glass
or my teen daughter
seeing my yoga pants
    (the purple ones that don't
make me look fat)
exclaiming: "Mom, you're so random!"
    (is this a *dis*?
or a *wicked sick* compliment?)

    The flowers arrayed
in our devil-may-care garden
riots of colour strewn in sudden tufts
    the kids' playthings tossed
willy-nilly on the porch
    a stone skipping
thirteen times across the bay
    and all the vanishing honeybees
or why an insult stings my throat
this moment
but wouldn't have last night

Patterns of stars fixed in the cosmos
like a giant sneezed them into space
    how they stick there
and we on this tiny planet
specks of sand on a galactic beach
    and me just happening to be here
wondering why I'm randomly writing
    about randomness.

The Inner Wisdom of Objects

for Pat Schneider

How woollen coats slump
on the hook after a rough day at school.

How nubbly socks pick up crumbs
from the polished floor and leave them elsewhere.

How pop bottle-caps leave
crown grooves in the dirt.

The newspaper opens itself by the heater
where the cat can nap on it.

The cat's water dish seems to divine a circle
on the kitchen floor like a signature.

A signature betrays quirks of personality
with a scribble or a dash.
The smallest squiggle becomes
a fused egg, a newborn, an infant.

A breathing object who grows up to hang his coat,
slide on sleek floors, flip and flatten
bottle-caps into the earth, a pattern
that might catch a poet's eye.

This paper has a tenderness
for the scratch and flow of pen
the scrawlof lines and circles —
a seal floating on its smooth skin.

About The Author

Kate Marshall Flaherty is published in journals such as *Descant*, *CV2*, *Freefall*, and *Windsor Review*. She was short-listed for Nimrod's Pablo Neruda Poetry Prize, the Malahat Review Long Poem and Descant's Best Canadian Poem. She lives in Toronto with her husband and three spirited children, where she guides yoga/retreats/writing workshops. Poetry is her lifeline.

Credits

"Goose, Plummeting", "Triptych for One Loon" and "Practicing Like Water" are to be made into film at Poetry Storehouse, as part of *Verse in Motion*.

"Drumming, For Nelson Mandela" was first published in *Modern Morsels*, McGraw-Hill 2011.

"How to Slice a Mango" and "Skin" first appeared in *Crave It: Food Anthology* by Red Claw Press, 2011.

"On Locky, Leaning Closer" first appeared in *Malahat Review*, 2011 and was short-listed for the *Malahat Review* Poetry Contest, 2011.

"Apocalypse of Bees" first appeared in *Descant*, as Honourable Mention in the Winston Collins Poetry prize, 2011.

"Skrimhold of Reve and other poems" was shortlisted in *Malahat Review*'s Long Poem Prize, 2011.

"Goose, Plummeting" won Honourable Mention in the Merton Poetry of the Sacred Contest, 2011.

"Photograph" first appeared in *Descant*: Prison Issue, 2011.

"Lining up Ducks" won Honourable Mention in the Robert Frost Poetry Contest, 2010.

"White Sheets", "Next of Kin" and "Practicing Like Water" first appeared in *Saranac Review*, 2010.

"Far Away" was also shortlisted in the Descant Winston Collins Poetry Prize, 2010 and then appeared in *Dream Catcher*: Canadian Poetry Issue, 2009.

"What is Bagged in the Shed" was entitled "As A Child" and won Honourable Mention for *CV2*'s Two-Day Poem Contest, 2008.

"When the Kids are Fed" won first prize in *THIS Magazine*'s Great Canadian Literary Hunt, 2008.

Printed in January 2014
by Gauvin Press,
Gatineau, Québec